GO FACTS FOOD
Farms

A & C BLACK • LONDON

Farms

© Blake Publishing 2003
Additional material © A & C Black Publishers Ltd 2005

First published 2003 in Australia by Blake Education Pty Ltd

This edition published 2005 in the United Kingdom by
A & C Black Publishers Ltd, 37 Soho Square, London W1D 3QZ
www.acblack.com

ISBN-10: 0-7136-7276-5
ISBN-13: 978-0-7136-7276-3

A CIP record for this book is available from the British Library.

Written by Paul McEvoy
Design and layout by The Modern Art Production Group
Photos by John Foxx, Photodisc, Brand X, John Deere Ltd p16, Corbis,
Digital Stock, Eyewire and Artville.

UK series consultant: Julie Garnett

Printed in China by WKT Company Ltd.

A & C Black uses paper produced with elemental chlorine-free pulp,
harvested from managed sustainable forests.

What is a Farm?

A farm is a place where crops or animals are raised for food or other uses. Most of the food we eat comes from farms.

Plants raised on farms are called crops. Some farmers grow food crops, such as fruits, grains and vegetables.

Most animals raised on farms are called **livestock**. Livestock provide foods such as meat, milk and eggs. They also give us wool and leather.

Sweetcorn

Australia has more than 140 000 farms.

Dairy cows are milked twice a day.

Fruits

Some farmers grow fruit. Fruit can grow on trees, vines or bushes.

Apples, peaches and oranges all grow on trees in orchards. Fruit trees are **pruned** to produce the most fruit and to make the fruit easy to pick. Most fruit is still picked by hand.

Apples, pears and berries need cool winters to grow well. Oranges grow best in countries where it is sunny and warm. Orange trees can die if they freeze in winter. Fruits such as bananas and pineapples grow only in very warm, **tropical** countries.

Pineapple plants

Large orchards, like this pear orchard, can have hundreds of trees.

Bananas grow in large bunches.

Strawberries are packed by hand into boxes in the field.

Vegetables

Some farmers grow vegetables. They grow different crops depending on the season and the climate.

Many vegetables need a certain temperature to grow well. Some vegetables that grow well in cooler weather are carrots, onions, and spinach. Tomatoes, cucumbers and peppers need hot, sunny weather to grow well.

Potato harvest

Some vegetables, such as lettuce, are quick growing. Lettuce is ready to eat in six to eight weeks. Other vegetables, such as tomatoes and sweetcorn, take four to five warm months to grow and ripen.

Cucumbers grow best in light, sandy soil.

Cabbages grow best in moist soil with a lot of nutrients.

Farmers choose crops that grow well in their area.

9

Grains and Other Crops

Farmers around the world grow more grain than any other crop. Farmers grow some crops to make drinks, seasonings and fabric.

Grains, such as wheat, rice, corn and oats, are very important crops. Grains are made into breakfast cereals or into flour for breads and pasta.

Farmers grow some plants for their special flavours. They grow basil and other herbs for their tasty leaves.

Cotton is an important crop that isn't grown for food. It is grown and harvested to make fabric for clothes, and sheets.

Cotton plant

10

Corn is planted in rows.

Farmers need dry, warm weather for harvesting cotton.

Wheat is grown in very large fields.

Cows and Sheep

Some farmers raise herds of cattle. Others raise flocks of sheep.

Farmers raise herds of cows, called **cattle**, for their meat and **hides**. Leather is made into shoes, clothes and furniture. Cattle eat grass in fields, or are fed hay and grain.

Dairy cows make milk. Milk can be made into cheese, yoghurt and ice-cream.

Farmers raise sheep for their wool, meat and milk. Farmers **shear** sheep once a year. The wool can be made into jumpers, blankets and carpet.

Shorn sheep

Cows graze in large fields.

Sheepdogs help farmers to round up sheep.

GO FACT!

DID YOU KNOW?

A cow can give 200 000 glasses of milk in her milking life.

Sheep grow thick, woolly coats.

13

Other Farm Animals

Many other animals, including horses, chickens, pigs and goats, are raised on farms.

For many years horses were used for most of the work on farms. Today, in some countries they are still used to round up sheep and cattle

Goats

Poultry, such as chickens, ducks and turkeys, are raised for their meat or eggs.

Pigs and goats are raised for their meat and hides. Goats' milk can be used to make yoghurt and cheese.

Farms where horses are raised are called stud farms.

GO FACT!

HOW LONG?

A hen takes 24 to 26 hours to produce an egg. After 30 minutes, she starts all over again.

Hens lay eggs in a chicken coop.

Some farmers raise fish in special ponds.

15

Farm machines do many of the jobs that used to be done by hand.

Tractors do many jobs on farms, such as moving hay and food for animals. Tractors pull machines that dig up the soil, plant seeds and pick crops.

Combine **harvesters** are large machines that cut and sort tonnes of grain a day. Many vegetables and cotton are also harvested using machines.

Farmers use special buildings. Barns protect animals and store hay. Some farmers grow crops inside **greenhouses**.

Tractor

A shearer takes about three minutes to shear a sheep.

These harvesters are cutting hay.

The temperature inside a greenhouse is controlled by the farmer.

Crops

Livestock

18

Glossary

cattle	cows raised on a farm
greenhouse	heated glass building used to grow plants
harvester	a machine that harvests or picks crops
hide	the skin of an animal
livestock	animals grown for food
poultry	birds raised for meat or eggs
prune	cut branches to shape a tree
shear	cut the wool off
tropical	warm all year round

Index